# Toilet Awareness

Using Montessori Philosophy to create a Potty Learning Routine

Second Edition

## Sarah Moudry

# Toilet Awareness

# TABLE OF CONTENTS

# Introduction

For a young child, their daily routine changes drastically the day you introduce potty-training. Many parents worry about what this means emotionally for their child. I encourage you to not worry about the transition and rather consider what a great opportunity this is to introduce new self-care skills to your child. This is a step your child is capable of making, and is a normal process for a human to go through. Children respond to the environment that is prepared for them. When you create a supportive environment for learning to use the toilet, your child will respond naturally and proceed at his own natural pace. His pace will depend on many things such as:

- Physical development: if your child cannot walk or doesn't ever seem to stop running, he will rely on you to get him to the bathroom. This does not mean he is not 'ready'; it simply means this is a part of the process that you will need to be more involved in.

- His understanding and control of his own body: when children first move from diapers to underwear, they must learn the connection between a full bladder, the release, and the uncomfortable feeling of wet underwear. It takes time to put these pieces together. It does not mean that he is not 'ready', it just means he needs time to understand.

- Access to the bathroom: a well-prepared bathroom space will help support your child's success in this process. If the bathroom is consistently maintained in the same way, this will make the process easier for your child to participate and internalize.

- Role modeling of proper bathroom use by other children and parents: seeing the toilet used by others helps a child to understand its purpose.

- Consistency: Your child will rely on you to be as consistent as possible as you start this new routine. He will internalize the process with time and practice and will rely on you to offer that consistency until then.

# Defining Toilet Awareness

Toilet awareness is when a person is aware of the toilet, how to use it, the body functions that are required, and the sensations that signal when to use the toilet.

There are four key elements involved in the child's toilet awareness:

1. He must have exposure to an orderly bathroom and a consistent routine for bathroom use.

2. He needs regular opportunity to practice using the bathroom.

3. He needs to see other people use the bathroom correctly and successfully to have a full understanding of how to use it.

4. He must trust the adults to support this process and will then trust in the process of toileting.

# Signs of Readiness

Many parents ask, "How do I know when my child is ready to start?" From a Montessori perspective, there are four steps to knowing what is developmentally appropriate for your child (including for learning to use the toilet):

1. Understand typical development;
2. Prepare the environment;
3. Observe your child;
4. Adjust the environment accordingly.

When we take these steps in preparing for Toilet Awareness, we see that a child is ready for a toileting routine as early as birth, and ready for independent toileting when they are walking. In order to create a supportive environment for toileting, you will need to consider both the emotional and physical environments.

## 1. Understand the Development

Intellectually, a child needs a supportive environment to begin to understand his bodily functions. This can start at birth. Creating this environment starts with talking to your child. Explain to him what is happening during his diaper change. He will learn from you the names of his body parts and their functions. You will provide him with the framework for understanding his body. Once his sphincter muscles are ready, he can begin to make choices to use those muscles at the appropriate time.

Physically, a child is ready to independently start using the toilet once his muscles and nervous system have developed. Typically, the sphincter muscles are ready at around the age a child can walk. Although the muscles may be fully developed, they need practice and exercise to be voluntarily controlled. This book offers the details on how to help your child gain control of those muscles.

A child must also have the opportunity to connect the sensation of a full bladder with the release of urine. This happens when a child wears cloth diapers or cotton underwear. The natural fibers allow the child to feel wet, rather than wicking the wetness away.

A child knows this feeling of wetness is uncomfortable and should be changed right away. He then learns that the body's normal state is clean and dry.

## 2. Prepare the Environment

Emotional Environment

In order to create a prepared emotional environment, you will need to be aware of your own opinions of potty training, urinating and bowel movements. Children can often sense the feelings of their parents, even when the parent does their best to hide them. Before the age of three, a child learns appropriate and acceptable reactions and responses from the adults around him.

Thus, it is important to use positive language when talking with your child about his toileting. It is from your attitudes and expressions that he will learn to feel comfortable with his normal bodily functions. It is essential that he feels comfortable and relaxed through the process so that he does not withhold his urine or bowel movement, which can lead to other challenges.

The more relaxed you can be, the more relaxed your child will be. When your child is successful in getting his urine or bowel movement in the toilet, you can say, without emotion, "you put your urine in the toilet." There is no need for praise such as clapping or stickers. Your child will feel a natural pride for having been successful and giving praise only sets you up to reproduce the situation in order to receive an external reward.

This is not a small point. You are supporting your child's natural development including learning to use the toilet. Using the toilet is expected of all typically developed humans in our society. Your child is joining the rest of our culture by learning to use the toilet. Praise sends the message that he has done something extraordinary and communicates that perhaps you were not sure that he could do it.

Certainly, these are proud moments as a parent. It is exciting to see your child making the connections in getting the routine. Smile internally and let your child have the moment. Don't steal it away with your own celebration; let him decide how he feels about the moment. Then celebrate in private (with your co-parent).

When your child misses the toilet, don't shame him or use negative language. This is just as important as not using praise. Again, treat it as just another moment in the day. Without judgment, state what happened, "I see that your urine is on the floor. We need to clean up the urine and you need dry underpants." In both situations, it is important to use a matter-of-fact tone of voice.

Another important note to make about the emotional environment touches on the language you use when discussing bodily functions. Use a matter-of-fact tone and clear language when you notice an odor from a bowel movement. For example, "I smell that you may have some gas," or "your bowel movement has a strong odor today."

It is just fine to recognize the situation as your child may also have noticed, but may not know the appropriate reactions. However, saying something such as "Whew, you are stinky!" may work against you and hinder your child's effort and toileting. A child may feel ashamed or discouraged from such messages.

Physical Environment

The space where your child will learn to use the toilet must be well prepared. This means that you must spend time looking at and evaluating the space before you introduce the toilet to your child. Small aspects of the environment can be modified later; consistency in the environment creates a consistent routine.

You will need:

- ❏ A toilet — also called a potty chair; simple in style and design, no gimmicks, should not sing nor light up, easy to use, comfortable
- ❏ Sink
- ❏ Step stool to the sink — this allows your child independence in washing his hands after he uses the toilet. (Making hand washing part of the routine from the beginning will lay the foundation for it to always be part of the process.)
- ❏ Soap — a small hotel-size soap or liquid soap dispenser
- ❏ Hand towel — ensure this is within reach of your child (consider adding a low hook or towel bar within reaching distance of your child). Fingertip towels or washcloths are often the best size for small hands.
- ❏ Wipes/toilet paper — toddlers are fond of unrolling toilet paper and pulling wipes out of the box. To keep your child from using all of the toilet paper or wipes in one use, place only a few in a basket

or reusable wipes container and keep the larger supply out of reach. Refill as needed to support independence and toileting.

❏ Hamper for soiled clothes — it is essential that you designate a space for wet and soiled clothing. There will be masses and your child needs to understand where these items go once he removes them.

❏ Basket with clean underwear — also essential to this process is your child's ability to choose and put on his own clean underwear. Having a basket or drawer close by with a supply of clean underwear will support this process.

> *"The child builds his innermost self out of the deeply held impressions he receives."*
>
> -Dr. Maria Montessori

Other items you may want:

❏ Rug or skid-proof mat under the toilet — this can help with near misses and keep the toilet from sliding while your child is using it

❏ Art on the wall — this helps create a space in which it is desirable to spend some time. In the beginning, you and your child may be spending a good amount of time in the bathroom, and hanging a child-sized piece of art helps to beautify the environment and show that care has gone into preparing the space.

❏ Dressing stool — a stable place for your child to sit while dressing and undressing

❏ Adult stool — a low stool where you can sit while your child uses the toilet

❏ Carpet cleaner

❏ Towels for wiping up the floor

A well-prepared space sends the message, "I support your process and I'm here to help you as you learn how to use the toilet."

Once your environment is prepared, you are ready to introduce the routine of Toilet Awareness. You can then observe how your child takes to the process; what you see will guide how you adjust the environment. Tips for observing and making adjustments are in *The Process* (page 19)

*"To assist a child we must provide him with an environment which will enable him to develop freely."*

-Dr. Maria Montessori

# The Language You Use

It is important to use the correct language in all aspects of your child's life. When you speak with your child, get down on his level, speak clearly and deliberately, without baby talk, and without modified words.

Using correct language will support your child's need to know the name for each thing in his environment. As his brain develops, he is curious to know the name of each object in his world. Learning the correct words for those items helps him have a full grasp of his language and be successful in his attempts to communicate with others.

In early language development, children use single words to represent general groups of names for things. For example, a child will call all animals that walk on four legs "dog." Later, as he learns more animal names and can differentiate between them, he will start to use other names such as cow and giraffe.

As his language develops, he struggles if multiple words are used to describe the same object or action. This is why it is key for the adults in his life to offer consistency in language.

When baby talk or modified language is used, a child will have to relearn later when the correct language is offered. For example, many parents use the term 'baba' instead of 'bottle.' Although your child may naturally say 'baba,' this is his best approximation of when you say bottle. He still wants to hear the correct pronunciation and in time will be able to match the pronunciation.

If the correct language is not offered as a model, he may become frustrated when he tries to communicate with others who use different modified language or simply do not understand him.

For example, when a child learns to describe the release from his bladder as 'urinating,' he can then, with confidence, inform any adult in his environment that he needs to urinate when he feels the sensation, and they will understand.

Learning to use the toilet is another opportunity to teach your child the correct and consistent words for the parts of his body, the functions of the body, and the items used for caring for the body. Children will use the language that is offered to them. The only shortcut to correct language is to always model correct language.

Using baby talk or modified language can delay the process of developing complete language and can require extra developmental energies that could be more useful for other aspects of development.

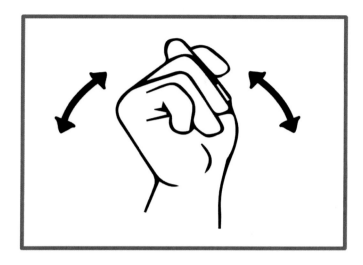

Another way to support your child's ability to express his need is offering sign language. Receptive language develops earlier than expressive language, meaning; a child understands much more than he is able to express. Show your child the sign language for toilet by making the sign for 't' with your hand and then rotating your wrist back and forth. When you make the sign, say 'toilet.' Do this every time you offer the opportunity for your child to sit on the toilet. He will begin to associate the word, the action, and the sign. He can then begin to sign to you when he needs to use the toilet.

# The Importance of Independence

When a person is independent, he feels an inner pride that serves the development of a positive self-image that can only be developed from within. Creating a positive self-image of oneself in the first three years of life (before social awareness) lays the foundation of self-love.

The best way for your child to learn to love himself, is to know in the core of his being that he is innately good, capable, and loved. These feelings come from a strong support system around him that allows him to do things for himself, whether he fails or succeeds. This support system is there to assist when he cannot do it for himself.

A young child is just developing independence and often needs collaborative efforts to accomplish these tasks. This often means that an adult can be nearby when he is trying to put his underwear on, but the help he needs is not to hold his underwear for him but to be shown how to hold the underwear open while he tries to get his feet through each hole.

Teaching these skills takes time from the parent and reassurance to the child. Depending on your child's personality, he may need more time or less. Say to him 'yes, you can do it. I will hold one side and you hold the other.' Once the underwear is on his feet, ask him to stand up. Now say 'pull up your underwear in the front, and I will pull in the back.' Work together and in no time your child will be doing this on his own.

*Any child who is self-sufficient, who can tie his shoes, dress, or undress himself, reflects in his joy and sense of achievement the image of human dignity, which is derived from a sense of independence."*

-Dr. Maria Montessori

# Clothing for Independence

**Underwear**

For daytime training when you are at home and in a familiar setting, use all-cotton training pants that will feel wet to your child when he urinates.

**Underwear Basics**

**Fabric content**: It is important to choose underwear made from natural fibers such as cotton, bamboo, and/or hemp. These are all soft and comfortable and allow your child's skin to breathe. Underwear made of polyester and other synthetic fibers trap the moisture against the skin and can cause rash and irritation.

**Fit:** As your child starts to use the toilet it is important that he has as much control over the process as possible. The goal is to support him to become independent in the bathroom, so allowing for as much independence as possible, as early on as possible, conveys your respect for your child's process and need to care for himself. In order to best support this step, choose underwear with a proper fit:

- Easy for your child to pull up and down
- Not too tight in the waist or the legs
- Not too loose in the waist

**Three Types of Underpants**

1. Simple cotton, no padding underwear.
2. Training Underpants
3. Travel Training Underpants

## 1. Simple cotton, no padding underwear

These can be used during the day and are made of 100% cotton. The less clothing/fabric, the greater the success. This is true for many children. Using bulky or padded training pants can trigger a muscular memory for your child. This means that when they feel the  bulk between their legs, their bladder naturally releases. This happens because they are used to wearing a diaper where bulk between the legs is the typical experience.

If a child wears lightweight no bulk cotton underwear, he has a greater connection to the feeling of a full bladder and a controlled release. This allows him to be more aware of his need to use the toilet. Many parents will often allow their child to be bare-bottomed while at home during early toilet training for just this reason.

## 2. Training pants

These underpants are designed to be thicker and more absorbent between the legs. This is done through the use of more layers of fabric or a sponge inside the layers  of fabric. These can work well for families that are concerned about puddles around the house but may slow the process of potty-training as they are bulkier between the legs and more difficult to pull on and off.

### 3. Travel training pants

These can be just the thing when you are on the go. These underpants have a cotton interior and a waterproof outer layer. They will often hold one bladder release. This can be helpful when you are at a store or in

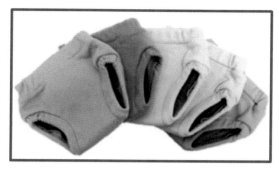

the car and unable to get to a bathroom right away. They pull up and down like regular underpants, but are bulky and can feel much like a diaper to your child. The benefit to using the travel training pants instead of a disposable "pull-up" is that a child still feels the 'feedback' of being wet and uncomfortable after releasing the bladder; a key factor in becoming aware of the need to use the toilet.

### T-shirts

It should easily fit over the child's head with no snaps or buttons at the neck. Cotton knit T-shirts work well. No onesies.

### Pants

Easy to pull on, elastic waist pants or shorts are perfect; your child can easily pull them up and down. Snaps and zippers make this process more difficult.

### Dresses and skirts

Dresses and skirts should be avoided as they are difficult to manage during toileting. Due to the extra fabric in dresses and skirts, they can hinder movement and frustrate the toileting process.

## — Note —

*Using disposable diapers or "pull-ups" will hinder the toilet awareness process and will probably make it take longer. Using disposables at some times but not others is a confusing message to your child and will prolong the toileting process.*

# The Process

1. Choose a day to start the toileting process.
2. Have the environment prepared and all the items that you will need for the process.
3. When your child wakes in the morning, take him to the prepared area and say, "today you are going to start using the toilet."
4. Name all of the items in the prepared area, "this is a hamper for soiled clothes. This is the toilet. These are the wipes."
5. Say to your child, "first we need to remove your underwear" or diaper, depending on whatever he is wearing.
6. Help your child remove his underwear by showing him how he can put his thumbs inside the waistband on each side. Tell him to push down. Work with him to push them all the way down.
7. Have him sit on the dressing stool to take one foot out of his underpants, and then the other.
8. Point to the hamper and say, "place your soiled underwear here."

9.  Have him take the underwear to the hamper. If he does not want to, you can do it for him. Don't demand that he does it, as it can become a power struggle and that can disrupt the process. Most children want to put their underwear in the hamper as they enjoy watching it fall in and the top swing back and forth.

10. Point out the toilet and say, "sit here on the toilet."

11. Once he is sitting, give him a moment to settle in. You can say, "if you feel pressure in your bladder, that is your urine you can push it out into the toilet." This is a new idea for him and he may not understand it immediately. Always offering the idea will help him get used to it and become familiar with the language and the process.

12. If he urinates in the toilet, ask him to move to the dressing area, while you empty the toilet. He will probably want to watch this process, and maybe even participate. It is important that he be involved as much as you are comfortable with, as this is his process.

13. Show him the basket of clean underwear. Say, "this is your clean underwear. You can wear these. If you need a fresh pair, they will be in here."

14. Show him how to put on his underwear by holding the sides with his thumbs and putting one foot in at a time.

15. Once he has both feet in, ask him to stand up and pull the underwear up in front. Say, "you pull in the front and I will pull up in the back." Work together to pull up the pants.

16. Go to the sink and help him wash his hands.

17. Tell your child there will be many opportunities to use the toilet throughout the day. He can use the toilet whenever he wants.

Many children like to repeat the process over and over again when it is new. Allow your child to do this, as this is his way of figuring it out.

Repeat the full process of removing underwear and sitting on the toilet:

- Every hour during awake hours
- When there is a mess (your child has wet underwear)

It is important that your child understand the proper use of the toilet area from the beginning. This sets the stage for a successful toileting experience. Do not let your child put the clean underwear in the hamper nor play with the toilet in the sink or other areas. Also, do not entertain your child while he sits on the toilet.

Convenient times to take your child to the toilet area include:

- After waking
- After a meal
- Before going outside
- When changing clothing
- Before a bath
- Between play activities
- Just before bed

**Observe and Adjust**

Now that you have offered the initial introduction of the toileting area, proceed every day with the toileting routine. You may find that your child can hold his urine longer than an hour and only needs to go about every two hours. Adjust as you learn your child's needs.

You may find that this all happens very easily and then all of a sudden after a week or two, your child regresses. This is normal. It is important that you continue with the same routine. This is your child's way of testing the boundaries and checking to see that he can trust that this is the expectation every day. Continue as before, without judgment or frustration and you will get through it together.

There is never a need to force your child to sit on the toilet. However, there may be times when your child resists. It is important that you let your child know that you have the same expectations and that he is expected to sit on the toilet. You can do this by pulling his underwear down, and having his bottom touch the toilet and pulling his underwear back up. Be open to the idea that he may at any moment want to join in, or that he may be mad at you. That is all normal. Tell him, "maybe next time you will have some urine to push out."

Consistency and routine are what allow a child to take control of his own toileting process. When he feels empowered to control his bodily functions, he will be successful.

# Taking It on the Road

Once you start the toileting process, the idea of leaving the house can be a little overwhelming. Here are a few tips that may help.

1. Start with short outings to get both you and your child used to being away from the house.
2. Have your child sit on the toilet before you leave the house.
3. Use training pants. There are many options available. Look for reusable 'training pants' with a waterproof outer layer, and an all cotton, hemp, or bamboo inner layer.
4. Put a towel or a 'piddle pad' on the car seat.
5. At each place you arrive, tell your child, "they have a bathroom here. If you feel that your bladder is full, tell me and we will go to the bathroom."
6. Take extra clothes.
7. Take plastic bags to hold wet clothes.
8. Use public restrooms and let go of any fears. Your child needs to learn how to use the public restrooms.

# Toileting From Birth

If you are interested in introducing the toilet before your child is walking, there are a few things to consider. Here are a few tips, combined with the *Toilet Awareness* method described in this book, that will support you and your baby as you go through this learning process.

**Read your baby**

You are learning to read your baby signs and you should have little to no expectation that he is able to control his sphincter muscles before he is walking. It is important to understand your baby's signals. Many 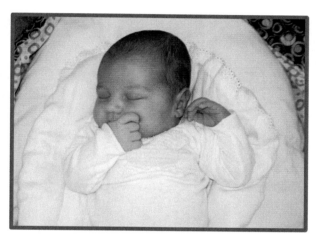 babies will squirm or cry just before releasing their bladder, while others will do this just after. A good way to determine your pre-crawling child's signals is to create a free-play time in your day when your baby can lay flat on a mat or blanket without a diaper. Place a few toys around him and hang a mobile above him just out of reach. Observe him and you may notice a few things:

- How often he urinates
- If he cries or scorns before urinating
- If he cries or screams after urinating

## Be at the ready

Another time to watch your child for signs is while he is eating. Babies have a gastro-colic reflex. This means when they eat, they have to go! Many babies can be held on the toilet just after eating and have a bowel movement in the toilet. Just keep the diaper loose and ready to be removed quickly.

## Use cloth diapers

Cloth diapers will help your child become familiar with the sequence of sensorial sensations that occur in the cycle of relieving the bladder.

1. First the feeling of dryness
2. Then the feeling of a full bladder
3. Then releasing the bladder
4. Then wetness
5. Then dryness again after a diaper change

Disposable diapers are meant to wick away the feeling of wetness. This has the long-term effect of prolonging the toileting process.

## Add language to the experience

Every time you change your child's diaper, bathe him or offer the toilet, give him correct language about his body and name his body parts. This helps connect the language with the actions.

## Show your child the sign language for toilet

Use the sign and say the word toilet every time you sit him on the toilet or change his diaper.

## Hold him on the toilet in a supportive way

Whether using a regular toilet or a potty chair, help your child feel secure. This may mean using one hand to support his legs and the other to support his torso and head. Find a supportive hold that works for both of you as your child will not be able to support his weight in a sitting position just yet.

**Offer the toilet at regular times in your routine**

- First thing in the morning
- Before a bath
- Every time you change his diaper

**Maintain expectations and approach the situation in a matter-of-fact tone**

Refrain from scolding or celebrating. Approach the situation always in a straightforward manner. This will convey the idea that this is a normal and healthy step in development.

**Be patient**

Every child has his own personality and therefore his own way of learning new things. If you stay patient and calm and toileting is a routine part of your day, he will happily oblige.

# Starting After Three

Introducing the toilet after your child turns three years old can have its own set of challenges. The need for routine and matter-of-fact tone from you is still essential. Additionally, an older child is able to converse with you more on the topic. It is key you approach this process as a normal expectation. Do not treat your child as if he is extraordinary for putting urine in the toilet, nor somehow bad for missing. This is a normal human activity. It will take time, no praise, much understanding, and patience.

Every child has a unique personality and therefore his own approach to mastering his body. This is a step along his way to autonomy. Some children take quickly to using the toilet, but others seem to take forever. Honor that this is your child's process, you cannot do it for him, and you can only make the conditions optimal for learning.

Add the following tips to the *Toilet Awareness* method described in this book to support your older child as he goes through this learning process.

**Understand what he is going through**

It is important to take a step back and imagine how his life is changing. The expectation for the last three years or so of his life has been that he can release his bladder or bowel any time or place and you will clean it up. Now you are changing the rules. The new expectation is that he goes in the toilet. It will take time for him to adjust.

Also, it takes time for him to make the connection between the signs his body gives that he needs to use the bathroom and actually acting on those feelings in a timely manner. Be patient.

**Maintain expectations and approach the situation in a matter-of-fact tone**

Let him know that he is to use the toilet when he needs to urinate or have a bowel movement and that you are there to remind him.

**Keep bathroom breaks as regular as possible**

It is best to add the bathroom break as a regular part of the routine; do not waver. Tell your child when it is time to use the toilet.

- Whenever you have a transition in the day
- Before leaving the house
- hen returning to the house
- Before a nap, after a nap
- Before a meal
- Before going outside to play

**Only use underwear**

Once you start the toilet awareness process, do not go back to diapers. Using diapers will only prolong the process and send mixed messages to your child. Use thin white cotton underpants. Bribing your child with superhero or princess underwear designs rarely works for more than a day and can give the parent false hope. Stick to the basics. Try not to use the potty chair. Once a child is in his preschool years, he is more socially aware. He may not be interested in using a designated potty chair and will instead prefer to use a seat that fits into a regular size toilet. Add a step stool to the toilet for his independence.

*"Only through freedom and environmental experience is it practically possible for human development to occur."*

-Dr. Maria Montessori

# Final Thoughts

- Regardless of whether there is a miss or a success, do not have judgment in your voice.
- Always offer the toilet in a matter-of-fact tone of voice.
- Never ask your child if he wants to sit on the toilet. Always state, "it is time to sit on the toilet." If you ask, he has the option to decline.
- Role modeling is an important teaching tool. It is important that your child see you use the toilet.
- Your child does not know what you are thinking. Verbalize your thoughts so he can understand your process. For example, say "I feel pressure in my bladder. I'm going to use the toilet now."
- Toileting is a skill that takes practice. There will be misses; be patient and know that your child will get there.
- Once your child has a routine down, give him the opportunity to go without a reminder. Test this every so often until he is able to do it.
- When children begin potty-training during the day it is important to still have a diaper or 'pull-up' during nap times and at night.

## When to seek outside help

If your child is older than 3 1/2 years and you truly have been consistent with the implementation for at least three consecutive weeks and you have seen no improvement, check with your pediatrician for a physical evaluation.

## When not to start toilet awareness

- Within a month of adding a sibling
- During a family crisis
- Just before or during a move
- Just before leaving for a vacation

# Recommended Reading

*In a Montessori Home*; Sarah Moudry NAMTA publications

*What is the Montessori Toddler Community;* Sarah Moudry, NAMTA publications

*Child in the Family*; Maria Montessori, Cleo (1992)

*Education and Peace;* Maria Montessori, Cleo (1992)

*Understanding the Human Being*; Silvana Quattrocchi Montanaro, Cleo (1992)

*The Montessori Toddler*; Simone Davies, Workman Publishing Company (2019)

*Montessori from the Start*; Paula Polk Lillard and Lynn Lillard Jessen, Schocken (2003)

*StudioJune.com*

*Aidtolife.org*

# What Parents Are Saying

*"I read Toilet Awareness and decided to just plunge into it. We were shocked how quickly our daughter took to the toilet awareness process. Days one and two were tough but then upon waking on day three, she literally just started using the toilet as if she always had been."*

-Carlie, mother of three

*"Sarah saved us months of frustration in potty-training our son. We had fewer accidents and completed the process much easier than with our daughter who learned a more traditional way. Sarah's straightforward approach allowed us to empower our son to learn the basics of toileting quickly and happily before he was two!"*

-Nikayla, mother of two

# What Teachers Are Saying

*"This book is fantastic! So well written, simple, and easy to read, understand, and follow. It goes exactly with what we do at school and more specifically what they should do at home! Wonderful!"*

-Corrina Vasquez, Oak Knoll Kinderhaus Montessori CA

*"This book allows me to communicate crucial information to parents without having to reinvent the wheel. Sarah offers the essential information in a clear and straightforward way that is easy to follow for parents entering the total bidding phase. Thanks, Sarah!"*

-Heather Moran, Children's Workshop MN

190613-2.2